CONSERVATIONISTS

JOHN MUIR

JOANNE MATTERN

ABDO Publishing Company

visit us at
www.abdopublishing.com

Published by ABDO Publishing Company, PO Box 398166, Minneapolis, MN 55439.
Copyright © 2014 by Abdo Consulting Group, Inc. International copyrights reserved in all countries. No part of this book may be reproduced in any form without written permission from the publisher. The Checkerboard Library™ is a trademark and logo of ABDO Publishing Company.

Printed in the United States of America, North Mankato, Minnesota.
112013
012014

 PRINTED ON RECYCLED PAPER

Cover Photo: Corbis, Getty Images
Interior Photos: Alamy pp. 7, 19; AP Images pp. 24, 25; Corbis pp. 17, 23, 27, 29; Getty Images p. 13; Glow Images pp. 14, 20; iStockphoto p. 19; Science Source p. 21; SuperStock p. 5; Thinkstock pp. 1, 15; Wisconsin Historical Society, WHS-2960 p. 6; Wisconsin Historical Society, WHS-40626 p. 9; Wisconsin Historical Society, WHS-68243 p. 11; Wisconsin Historical Society, WHS-32864 p. 11; Wisconsin Historical Society, WHS-4392 p. 17

Editors: Rochelle Baltzer, Megan M. Gunderson, Bridget O'Brien
Art Direction: Neil Klinepier

Library of Congress Cataloging-in-Publication Data

Mattern, Joanne, 1963-
  John Muir / Joanne Mattern.
      pages cm. -- (Conservationists)
  Includes bibliographical references and index.
  ISBN 978-1-62403-094-9
1. Muir, John, 1838-1914--Juvenile literature. 2. Naturalists--United States--Biography--Juvenile literature. 3. Conservationists--United States--Biography--Juvenile literature. 4. Environmentalists--United States--Biography--Juvenile literature. I. Title.
  QH31.M9M28 2014
  508.092--dc23
  [B]
                    2013030846

CONTENTS

A Scottish Lad

John Muir loved nothing better than to take long walks in the wilderness. He walked all over the United States and wrote about the beautiful things he saw. In time, he became one of the most well-known conservationists in America.

John lived most of his life in the United States, but he was born in Dunbar, East Lothian, Scotland. John was born on April 21, 1838. His parents were Anne Gilrye and Daniel Muir.

John was one of eight children in the family. John's brother David was just two years younger than he was. The two had many adventures together. They loved to walk through the fields and play near the North Sea.

John could already read when he started school at age three. Some of his earliest memories involved walks with his grandfather around this time. His grandfather would point out letters on signs and numbers on the town clock.

John's schoolteacher was **strict**, and John did not enjoy school. Yet he loved to read and learn new things. He also loved playing outside with the other boys after school. They enjoyed exploring the natural world all around them. They collected birds' nests and eggs, and even captured birds and set them free.

John Muir's last name is pronounced "MYUR."

TO AMERICA!

In February 1849, John's father came home with a surprise. He was moving the family to America! John, David, and their older sister Sarah would go with him right away. John's mother and other **siblings** would stay in Scotland until his father had built a new home for them.

Daniel Muir named the family's new home Fountain Lake Farm. The area they settled, including Fountain Lake, is now part of John Muir Memorial Park.

The Muir family sailed across the Atlantic Ocean for 45 days. Then they traveled across the United States. In May, the family settled in the woods of Wisconsin. They built a home and started a farm.

Farming was very hard work. The Muirs had to cut down trees, chop wood, and dig a well. They had to build fences, plow land, and plant crops, including corn, wheat, and potatoes.

They worked 16 hours a day, which left no time for school. John later wrote that the only time he did not have to work was when he got very sick with **pneumonia**. He had to stay in bed for weeks until he got better.

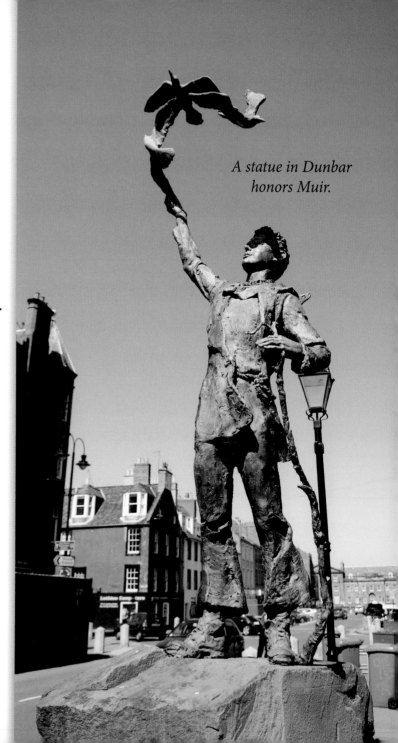

A statue in Dunbar honors Muir.

TIME TO HIMSELF

Despite all the hard work, John did find time to have a little fun. His father had promised to get a horse for John and David. He bought Jack for $13. The boys had fun riding Jack around the farm and in the woods. John loved exploring the wilderness and studying its animals and plants.

John and David also built a small boat to use on Fountain Lake. With that, they discovered fish and underwater plants.

John still loved to read. He even wanted to stay up late and read after his father went to bed. But his father said no. Instead, his father said he could get up as early as he wanted.

John loved this idea. He started getting up at one o'clock in the morning! John later said, "I can hardly think of any other event of my life, any discovery I ever made that gave birth to joy so . . . glorious as the possession of these five frosty hours."

On the edges of Fountain Lake, John shot muskrats. He sold their hides and used the money to buy more books.

FUN FACT:

Fountain Lake is also known as Ennis Lake and Muir Lake.

STUDENT INVENTOR

Muir also loved to invent things. When not reading, he spent some of his early-morning hours building machines. One invention was an "early rising machine." It was a special alarm clock set to tilt Muir's bed until he fell on the floor!

In September 1860, Muir decided to take some of his inventions to the Wisconsin State Agricultural Fair. It was an adventure!

Muir traveled by train to the capital city of Madison. He had $15 in his pocket. He took with him two clocks, a special thermometer, and his early rising machine. People at the fair loved Muir's inventions. He won prizes and was written about in the newspaper.

After the fair, Muir became an **apprentice** to an inventor in Prairie du Chien on the Mississippi River. Then he returned to Madison, where he began attending the University of Wisconsin. He took whatever classes interested him. A fellow student introduced him to botany, the study of plants. While at school, Muir invented a device to measure plant growth.

Muir never graduated from college. After a while, he decided to stop going to school. He later wrote that he left school to attend "the University of the Wilderness."

Two of Muir's clock inventions

FUN FACT:

To help pay for college, Muir taught in a nearby town. In the schoolhouse, he set up a clock device that started a fire each morning. That way, it was already warm when he arrived!

A Promise

Muir loved to explore nature, but he needed to make money too. Over the next few years, he worked at many different jobs. He traveled from place to place, including parts of Canada. Finally, he headed for Indianapolis, Indiana. He chose the city because it was surrounded by beautiful **deciduous** forests.

In 1867, Muir was working in a shop making wagon wheels. Suddenly, his hand slipped. The sharp tool he was holding stabbed him in the eye. Muir could not see out of his injured eye. Soon, he could not see out of his other eye either.

Muir had to rest in a dark room for many weeks. Fortunately, his eyesight came back after a few months. Muir never forgot this frightening time when he could not see the beauty of nature. He decided to spend the rest of his life exploring and enjoying everything nature had to offer.

Muir wanted to see the world! So he started to walk. Muir walked for a thousand miles, until he reached Florida. Then he got on a boat and sailed to the island of Cuba.

Next, Muir headed to California. He sailed to Panama and crossed the **isthmus**. Then he sailed up the coast to San Francisco. Muir was about to discover the place that would be close to his heart for the rest of his life.

The plants and animals Muir saw as he walked south were all new to him. He kept a journal and sketched what he saw along his way.

YOSEMITE

Muir had heard about Yosemite Valley, which is in the Sierra Nevada mountain range in California. He walked into it for the first time in April 1868. Muir had never seen anything like this majestic place. He wanted to learn all about it. To stay

Writing about the Sierras, Muir said, "We are now in the mountains and the mountains are in us."

nearby, he found several jobs, including one as a shepherd.

Muir kept working and studying Yosemite. On New Year's Day 1870, he climbed to the top of El Capitan, a huge rock structure at one end of the valley. And that year, he ran a sawmill and led tourists through the valley.

As Muir studied the valley, he became convinced it had been formed by glaciers cutting through the area. Many

Muir did not climb the side of El Capitan that faces the valley. It would be more than 80 years before anyone successfully climbed that face!

scientists disagreed. They thought the valley had formed when a huge earthquake struck the area.

To prove his idea, Muir pounded sticks into the ice to measure how much it moved. In time, he showed that glaciers were still shaping Yosemite.

In 1871, famous writer Ralph Waldo Emerson came to Yosemite. Muir was very excited to meet him and tell him about the valley. Emerson later encouraged Muir to leave Yosemite and teach the world about his discoveries. But Muir chose to stay. He kept working, learning, and writing.

FUN FACT:

Yosemite *is pronounced* "yoh-SEH-muh-tee."

TRAVEL & FAMILY

Muir did write about the Yosemite Valley. By the 1870s, he was published in many newspapers and magazines. People all over the world learned about nature by reading Muir's work.

Muir also traveled around other areas of the country. He climbed Mount Shasta in Northern California for the first time in 1874. There, he learned more about glacier formation by studying how snow falls. Muir also visited Utah several times and later Mount Rainier in Washington.

Muir took his first trip to Alaska in 1879. He became the first non-native person to discover Glacier Bay. Later, Alaska's Muir Glacier was named in his honor.

The day before he left for Alaska, Muir became engaged to Louisa Wanda "Louie" Strentzel. They married at Louie's family farm on April 14, 1880.

Louie and her parents lived on a large ranch with vineyards and orchards in Martinez, California. Muir moved to the ranch

Muir returned to the Alaskan glaciers in 1899 with fellow conservationist John Burroughs (left).

and helped run it for many years. He and Louie had two daughters. Annie Wanda, called Wanda, was born in March 1881. Helen was born in January 1886.

17

Wanda and Helen Muir

PRECIOUS SPACES

Besides studying mountains, valleys, and glaciers, Muir continued his lifelong love of trees. Like many people today, he was especially in awe of California's giant sequoia trees. Some are 3,000 years old! They are among the tallest and oldest living things on Earth.

Muir wanted to make sure that these special trees were always protected. He wrote about how they had stood the test

Giant sequoias tower over visitors to Mariposa Grove in Yosemite National Park.

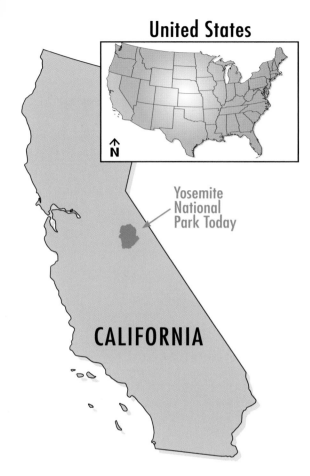

United States

Yosemite
National
Park Today

N

CALIFORNIA

of time, but were now in danger from humans. He felt only the US government had the power to protect them.

In 1864, President Abraham Lincoln had helped protect Yosemite Valley by giving it to the state of California. Meanwhile, lumbermen and ranchers had moved into the area around the valley. Their land use changed the landscape and affected the valley.

A larger area of land needed to be protected to save the valley and the sequoias. So, Muir wrote articles and gave talks. He explained how much damage was being done. Through a magazine editor, Muir got the attention of Congress, and Congress listened.

In 1890, Congress passed a law that protected the Yosemite Valley from grazing. Later that year, another law passed. It created Yosemite National Park surrounding the valley.

THE SIERRA CLUB

Muir served as president of the Sierra Club from 1892 until his death.

Muir knew there were many wild places in America that needed to be protected. So in 1892, he and some friends formed the Sierra Club.

The Sierra Club worked to protect Yosemite National Park. Members held meetings, presented educational talks, and organized trips to teach people about nature. Muir felt that people only had to see forests to want to protect them.

Not everyone agreed about exactly how to protect and conserve the wilderness. In 1896, Muir became friends with a conservationist named Gifford Pinchot. Later on, Pinchot said he thought it was okay to let sheep graze in forest preserves. Pinchot believed that natural resources should be carefully managed so they could be used by people and businesses.

Muir believed nature should be left alone. Because of this he was called a preservationist. Muir and Pinchot had many arguments. This **debate** over land use continues among **environmentalists** today.

Pinchot led the US Forest Service. The Gifford Pinchot National Forest in Washington is named for him.

THE PRESIDENT

Over the years, Muir met many important people. In May 1903, he found a lifelong friend in President Theodore Roosevelt. Roosevelt wrote Muir a letter asking him to take him on a camping trip. Roosevelt wished to drop politics for four whole days and simply explore the wilderness with Muir.

Roosevelt and Muir traveled deep into Yosemite. The first night, they slept among the towering giant sequoias in Mariposa Grove. The second night they stayed at Glacier Point, high above the valley. On the third night, they slept at the foot of El Capitan. As he showed the president around, Muir talked about how people were destroying the wilderness to make money.

Muir asked Roosevelt to protect the wilderness so people in the future could enjoy it. The president listened. Today, he is known for protecting 230 million acres (93 million ha) of land! He set aside land for many national parks and monuments.

After the camping trip, Muir left to travel the world. He visited France and Finland. He traveled across Russia. His

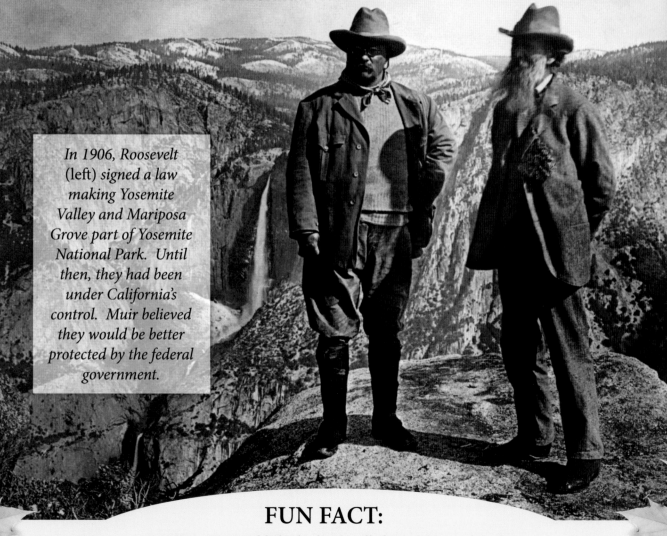

trip then took him to China, the Himalayas, Egypt, Australia, New Zealand, the Philippines, Japan, and Hawaii. Finally, he returned home to California.

In 1906, Roosevelt (left) signed a law making Yosemite Valley and Mariposa Grove part of Yosemite National Park. Until then, they had been under California's control. Muir believed they would be better protected by the federal government.

FUN FACT:

In 1901, Muir published a book called Our National Parks.

HETCH HETCHY

Hetch Hetchy Valley before 1913

Muir worked tirelessly to preserve the wilderness. One of his biggest battles was one he eventually lost.

Muir and the Sierra Club fought for years to save Hetch Hetchy Valley. Muir thought this valley was even more beautiful than Yosemite Valley. However, San Francisco was growing and needed more water. For some, damming the Tuolumne River in Hetch Hetchy Valley was the only answer. Muir argued there were other options.

President Roosevelt did not allow a dam to be built. Neither did the next president, William Howard Taft. However, Muir could not stop the dam forever. In 1913, President Woodrow Wilson signed a law saying the dam could be built.

Muir was very sad when he heard what President Wilson had done. The loss of Hetch Hetchy was hard for Muir to bear. "The Destruction of the charming groves and gardens, the finest in all California, goes to my heart," he wrote to a friend.

The O'Shaughnessy Dam created a reservoir in Hetch Hetchy Valley.

MUIR LIVES ON

Muir continued to write and spend time in Yosemite Valley until his death. In 1914, he got sick with **pneumonia** while visiting his daughter Wanda. He died in a hospital in Los Angeles, California, on December 24. Muir was buried near his home in Martinez.

Today, Muir is remembered as the "Father of Our National Park System." He worked hard to save America's wild places. Many national parks, including Yosemite, were created because of Muir's influence. Today, visitors to California can step into the John Muir Wilderness and Muir Woods National Monument.

CONSERVATION ALERT!

Today, some people want to restore Hetch Hetchy Valley. They believe the dam can be removed and new technology can be used to provide the water and power the dam now provides.

The Sierra Club also continues to work hard for what Muir believed in. Thanks to Muir's actions, millions of people became aware of nature's beauty and were inspired to save it.

Muir's home in Martinez

TIMELINE

1838 — John Muir was born on April 21 in Dunbar, East Lothian, Scotland.

1849 — Muir immigrated to the United States and settled in Wisconsin.

1867 — After an eye injury, Muir decided to spend the rest of his life exploring nature.

1868 — In April, Muir saw the Yosemite Valley for the first time.

1871 — Ralph Waldo Emerson visited Muir.

1879 — Muir traveled to Alaska for the first time.

1880 — On April 14, Muir married Louisa Wanda "Louie" Strentzel.

1881 — In March, Muir's daughter Annie Wanda was born.

1886 — In January, Muir's daughter Helen was born.

1890 — Congress passed a law to create Yosemite National Park.

1892 — Muir cofounded the Sierra Club.

1903 — Muir showed President Theodore Roosevelt the California wilderness.

1914 — On December 24, Muir died in Los Angeles, California.

PLACES NAMED IN HONOR OF JOHN MUIR

Muir Glacier, Muir Inlet, and Mount Muir in Glacier Bay National Park, Alaska

John Muir Highway, California

John Muir Branch Library, Los Angeles, California

Muir Woods National Monument, California

John Muir National Historic Site, Martinez, California

Muir Gorge, Yosemite National Park, California

Muir Valley, Kentucky

John Muir Nature Trail, New York City, New York

Muir Snowfield, Mount Rainier, Washington

Numerous schools and parks

Johnmuir, a minor planet in the Solar System

Under Muir Glacier

"Come to the woods, for here is rest."
—John Muir

GLOSSARY

apprentice - a person who learns a trade or a craft from a skilled worker.

debate - a discussion or an argument.

deciduous (dih-SIH-juh-wuhs) - shedding leaves each year. Deciduous forests have trees or shrubs that do this.

environmentalist - a person concerned with problems of the environment. The environment is all the surroundings that affect the growth and well-being of a living thing.

isthmus (IHS-muhs) - a narrow strip of land connecting two larger land areas.

pneumonia (nu-MOH-nyuh) - a disease that affects the lungs. It may cause fever, coughing, or difficulty breathing.

sibling - a brother or a sister.

strict - following or demanding others to follow rules or regulations in a rigid, exact manner.

WEB SITES

To learn more about John Muir, visit ABDO Publishing Company online. Web sites about John Muir are featured on our Book Links page. These links are routinely monitored and updated to provide the most current information available.

www.abdopublishing.com

INDEX